Pea Soup and the Seafood Feast

Happy reading!

Anna Burger

Pea Soup and the Seafood Feast

Written by Anna Burger
Illustrated by Laura Craig

BELLE ISLE BOOKS
www.belleislebooks.com

ISBN: 978-1-9399304-6-0
Library of Congress Control Number: 2015940911

BELLE ISLE BOOKS
www.belleislebooks.com

For Edward, and for Dad and Daddy Bill,
who taught me the ways of the water.

"I'm hungry!" Jack exclaimed.

"How can you be hungry? You just ate lunch," his mother replied.

Jack didn't know how, he just knew he was always hungry.

"You'll have to wait for dinner, Jack. We're having pea soup."

Jack's eyes grew wide. Gross! Jack hated pea soup. He would starve!

"I'm already hungry and Mom's serving pea soup for dinner. What will I do?" Jack wondered.

He looked in the refrigerator — empty! It was too far to walk to the store. Jack was getting worried. Tomorrow's breakfast seemed so very far away.

Then — an idea:

"A seafood feast!" Jack thought that was a very good idea indeed.

Jack grabbed his fishing rod. He fished often with his grandfather, but this would be his first time fishing on his own.

Jack gathered a cooler, bait, and his life jacket.

"I can't wait to tell Granddaddy about the seafood feast I catch!" thought Jack, and he ran down to the dock.

Jack found the line tied to the dock and slowly pulled the crab pot out of the water. He opened up the latch, slid a few pieces of chicken into the wire compartment, closed the pot, and tossed it back into the water.

"The crabs won't be able to resist this tasty chicken. When I come back, crabs for my seafood feast will be waiting for me!" Jack said.

Jack knew that he needed more than just crabs for his seafood feast. He snapped on his life jacket and hopped into his boat. Pulling hard on the cord to start the motor, Jack revved the throttle and off he went.

"Fish! I need fish for my seafood feast."

Jack rode away from his house and down the creek. He found the spot where he and his grandfather had fished together many times before, and he slowed his boat. With his trusty rod in hand, Jack pulled the slimy squid bait from the cooler, baited his hook, and cast out into the water.

Jack waited as he drifted along the channel edge. His tummy grumbled.

"What if I don't catch any fish?" Jack worried. "I just can't have pea soup for dinner. I'm already too hungry — I'll never make it to breakfast tomorrow!"

Suddenly, he saw the fishing line *tug tug tug* away from the boat. Jack gathered his strength and reeled in the line. A fish appeared out of the water and landed in his boat — a flounder!

He removed the hook and the flounder flopped its flat body around on the floor of the boat before Jack put it in the cooler.

"That flounder's sand-colored, spotted skin may camouflage it when it's lying flat on the bottom of the bay, but it can't hide from me," Jack thought as he studied the creature. "I'm glad my eyes aren't on the same side of my head like the flounder's eyes. What a funny-looking fish!"

Then Jack thought, "This flounder may be silly looking, but it's smart, too. Even when it's hiding on the bottom of the bay, it still has two eyes to look for bigger fish that might eat it. I think I'll let the flounder keep on using its camouflaged skin and funny eyes to hide. I can find another tasty fish for my seafood feast."

Jack tossed the flounder back into the water.

As his boat drifted into deeper water, Jack baited his hook and cast the line again.

A few minutes later, Jack felt another *tug tug tug*. He reeled in the line and a second fish landed in his boat.

Jack spied the one black dot near its gills — he had caught a spot! Jack laughed when he heard the spot's strange croaking sound: *Crooaak!*

"What a funny sound for a fish to make! I bet the other fish would like to hear it. They will laugh, too," Jack thought, and he slipped the spot back into the water.

"Fish are delicious, but I can have a feast without them," Jack decided. "Now, what else do I need? Clams! Of course! No pea soup for me!"

Jack started the boat's motor and sped over to the mud flats near his favorite beach.

He had been clamming with his grandfather before. He remembered how his grandfather taught him to look for little holes in the sand with bubbles coming out of them. Every bubbling hole meant a clam was breathing below the sand.

It was low tide now, and the mud was squishy between Jack's toes, but he knew there was a feast to be had under all that mud. He stuck his hand in the ground and pulled out a clam. Its smooth shell fit perfectly in the palm of his hand.

"Once I get home and cook this clam with my mother, its hard shell will open and the juicy meat inside will be delicious," Jack imagined, and he tossed the clam into his basket.

Jack's stomach was growling, so he kept working with his fingers and toes until he was completely covered in marsh mud. Still, Jack couldn't find any more clams! It was starting to get late, and the noises in his tummy were getting louder.

"One clam is not much of a feast," he decided, so he reluctantly returned the clam to its home.

"I'd better head home myself," Jack thought.

"No flounder, no spot, and no clams. I wonder if I will have any blue crabs. That would save my seafood feast!" Jack hopped back into his boat, revved the motor, and off he went.

Back at the dock, Jack pulled up his crab pot to find six dancing crabs inside. Their hard shells were muddy green, and their blue claws tipped with orange and white pincers grabbed at the air.

"I can't wait to tell Granddaddy that I caught six blue crabs all by myself," Jack thought as he watched them scramble around the pot.

Jack remembered his grandfather telling him that blue crabs are known as "beautiful swimmers" because of their speed and skill in the water.

"I wonder if they are better swimmers than me," Jack thought. He dropped one crab into the water and watched it swiftly kick its bright blue legs and swim under the dock.

"That was pretty good. I think I'll try another." Jack dropped a second crab into the water and that one also swam speedily away. "Wow! They really are beautiful swimmers!"

Jack continued releasing the crabs into the water and watched each one swim away until there were none left in the pot.

Empty-handed, Jack unloaded the boat and hurried up to his house. He couldn't wait to tell his mother about his adventure on the water.

"Oh, Jack, I was just starting to worry about you," his mother called from the porch.

"I was worried, too, Mom," Jack replied.

"What do you mean?" Jack's mother looked confused.

"I was worried about having to eat pea soup for dinner, so I went on a mission to find myself a seafood feast!" Jack's eyes gleamed. "I caught a flounder first, but it had done such a good job hiding from bigger fish with its camouflaged skin and both eyes on the same side of its head that I released it so it could hide some more.

"Next, I caught a spot, which made the funniest *Crooaak* sound." Jack's mother laughed as Jack croaked for her.

"I decided to let the spot go, too, so the other fish could hear the croaking."

"Then I went looking for clams but could only find one. I figured that wouldn't be much of a feast, but I had fun digging!"

"Yes, I see." Jack's mother frowned as she eyed his muddy clothes.

"After that, I caught six blue crabs in my crab pot, just like Granddaddy taught me!" Jack beamed.

"Well, where are they, Jack?" his mother asked.

"I let them go so I could watch them swim. They're really fast, Mom!" Jack told her. "So I don't have any crabs either."

"It sounds like you had a very fun day, Jack."

"I did, Mom, but there's just one problem," he replied. "After all this fishing and clamming and crabbing, I'm even hungrier than before!"

"You are? Well, what will you eat?" she asked.

"You know, I was thinking that pea soup doesn't sound so bad after all," Jack admitted.

Jack's mother smiled.

"I think pea soup sounds quite tasty, Jack.
I'll heat a bowl up for you."

About the Author

Anna Burger lives with her husband and young son on Virginia's Eastern Shore. She grew up on Onancock Creek, where she received her first boat at age 12 and learned how to crab and fish from her father and grandfather. After several years practicing law, she is now following her first love – writing.

About the Illustrator

Laura Craig was raised on the Eastern Shore of Virginia and currently lives with her husband and daughters in Fredericksburg. A hobbyist painter all her life, she is now a professional artist, and is excited to have her first opportunity to call herself an illustrator as well.

CPSIA information can be obtained at www.ICGtesting.com
Printed in the USA
BVOW07*0711031115

425305BV00001B/1/P

9 781939 930460